Community Helpers at Work

A Day in the Life of a
Veterinarian

by Heather Adamson

Consultant:
Daniel F. Simpson, DVM
West Bay Animal Hospital
Warwick, Rhode Island

Capstone press

Mankato, Minnesota

First Facts is published by Capstone Press,
1710 Roe Crest Drive, North Mankato, Minnesota 56003.
www.capstonepub.com

Library of Congress Cataloging-in-Publication Data
Adamson, Heather, 1974–
    A day in the life of a veterinarian/by Heather Adamson.
    v. cm—(First facts. Community helpers at work)
    Includes bibliographical references and index.
    Contents: What happens at the start of a veterinarian's day?—Do veterinarians
ever operate on animals?—What happens in an emergency?—Who helps veterinarians?
—Do veterinarians like animals?—Why do pets need to go to the veterinarian?—Do
veterinarians groom animals?—What happens at the end of a veterinarian's day?
    ISBN-13: 978-0-7368-2287-9 (library binding)
    ISBN-10: 0-7368-2287-9 (library binding)
    ISBN-13: 978-0-7368-4676-9 (softcover pbk.)
    ISBN-10: 0-7368-4676-X (softcover pbk.)
    1. Veterinarians—Juvenile literature. 2. Veterinary medicine—Vocational guidance—
Juvenile literature. [1. Veterinarians. 2. Occupations.] I. Title. II. Series.
SF756.A32 2004
636.089'092—dc21
                                                                      2002155832

Credits
Jennifer Schonborn, series and book designer; Gary Sundermeyer, photographer;
    Eric Kudalis, product planning editor

Artistic Effects
Capstone Press/Gary Sundermeyer; PhotoDisc

Special thanks to Dr. Kipling Jones-Lang and the Waseca Veterinary Clinic for their
    assistance in the photographing of this book. Thanks to Walter Mishek of the
    Arabian Horse Times for the use of his facilities and horse on pages 8–9.

Printed in the United States of America in North Mankato, Minnesota.
102015
009281R

Table of Contents

What happens at the start of a veterinarian's day?

Veterinarians arrive early at their clinics. Veterinarians care for animals. Dr. Kip checks on the animals that spent the night at the clinic. She looks at the day's appointments. Dr. Kip and the other clinic workers gather supplies and tools. Everything needs to be ready to use.

8:00 in the morning

Do veterinarians ever operate on animals?

Veterinarians operate almost every day. A team works together during an operation. Dr. Kip finds gowns, caps, and gloves for the team. These clothes protect against germs. An assistant gives the dog a shot so it will sleep. The dog will stay at the clinic until tomorrow.

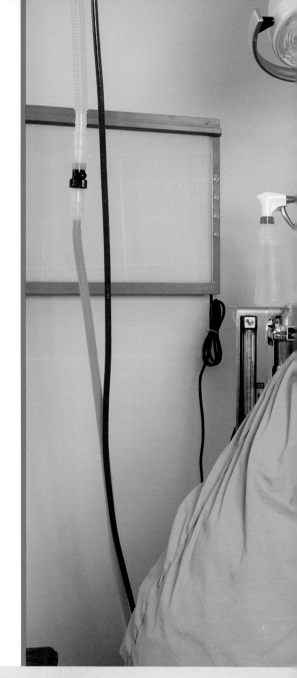

 Fun Fact:
Veterinarians and doctors who treat people need the same amount of medical school.

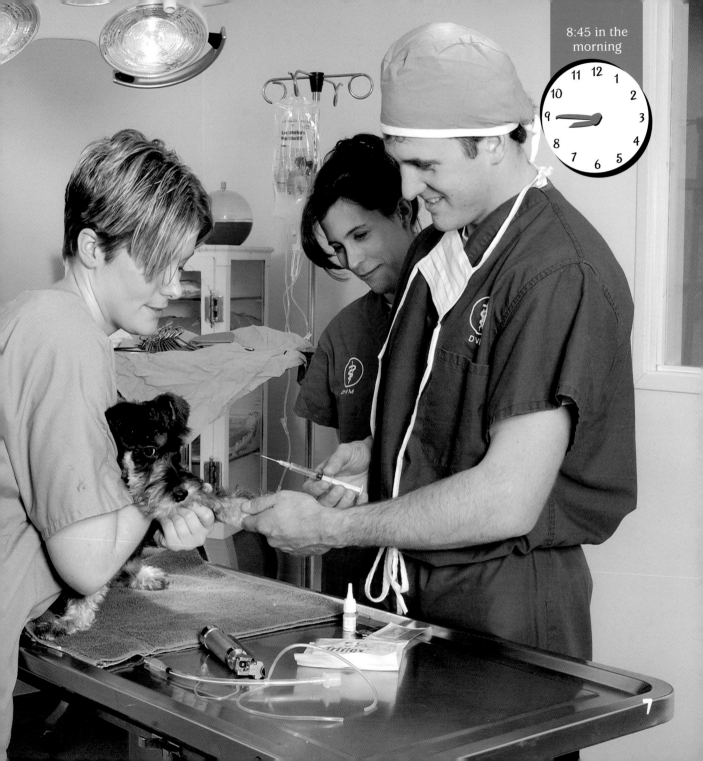

7

What happens in an emergency?

Veterinarians must be ready to help in an emergency. Mr. Mishek calls the clinic. His horse has cut its leg. Dr. Kip packs her medical kit.

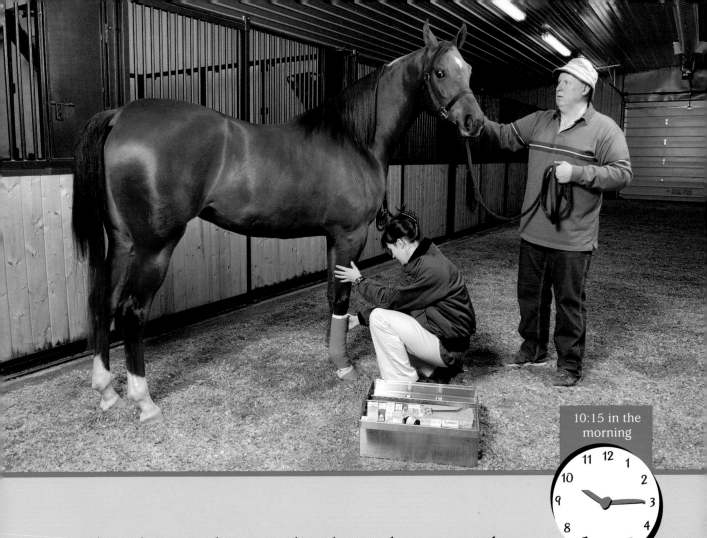

10:15 in the morning

She drives the medical truck out to the farm. She sews up the horse's cut and covers it with a bandage. The cut will heal in a few weeks.

Who helps veterinarians?

Veterinarians have assistants and technicians to help them. Dr. Kip's assistant helps weigh a big dog. The clinic also has workers who file records, set up appointments, and write out bills. Everyone works together to make the clinic run.

Do veterinarians like animals?

Veterinarians love all kinds of animals.
Dr. Kip checks the animals at the clinic.

1:00 in the
afternoon

She brings the dog some fresh water
and scratches its neck. She gives a
treat to a rabbit. Dr. Kip finds time to
eat her own lunch, too.

Why do pets need to go to the veterinarian?

Veterinarians help pets stay healthy and safe. Dr. Kip and a technician show a family how to take care of their cat. Dr. Kip gives the cat medicine. Now it will not catch diseases. Dr. Kip puts a tag on the cat's collar in case it gets lost. The tag helps the cat get returned to its family.

 Fun Fact:
Studies show that people with pets live longer than people without pets.

2:30 in the
afternoon

Do veterinarians groom animals?

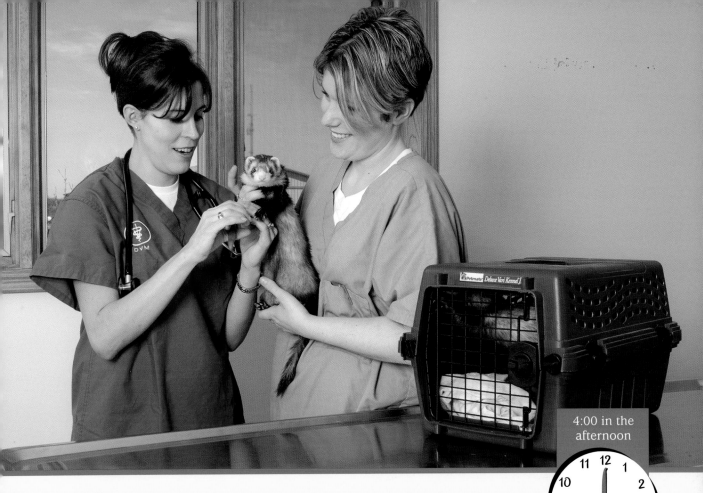

4:00 in the
afternoon

Veterinarians do some grooming tasks.
Today, Dr. Kip files a turtle's sharp beak.
She also cuts a ferret's nails. Veterinarians
do not usually trim fur. They do tell owners
how to keep their pets clean and healthy.

17

What happens at the end of a veterinarian's day?

Veterinarians make sure the clinic is clean. They check on the animals before they go home. Dr. Kip visits the dog that had an operation. Another worker will stay at the clinic until morning. Dr. Kip thinks about the animals she helped today. She is glad she is a veterinarian.

Fun Fact:

In the United States, more than 67,000 people work as veterinarians.

5:30 in the
evening

19

Amazing But True!

Zoonoses (zoh-uh-NOH-sez) are diseases that can spread from animals to people. Rabies and tuberculosis are zoonoses. Some veterinarians work in labs studying zoonoses. They find treatments to keep people and animals healthy.

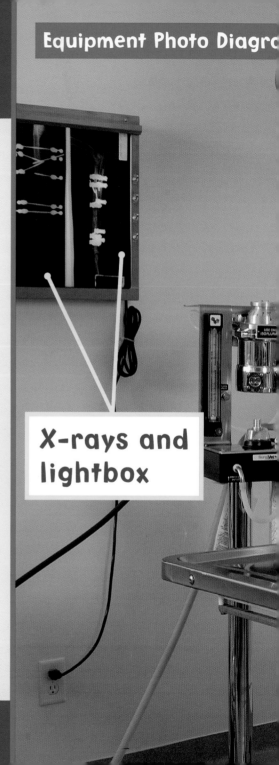

X-rays and lightbox

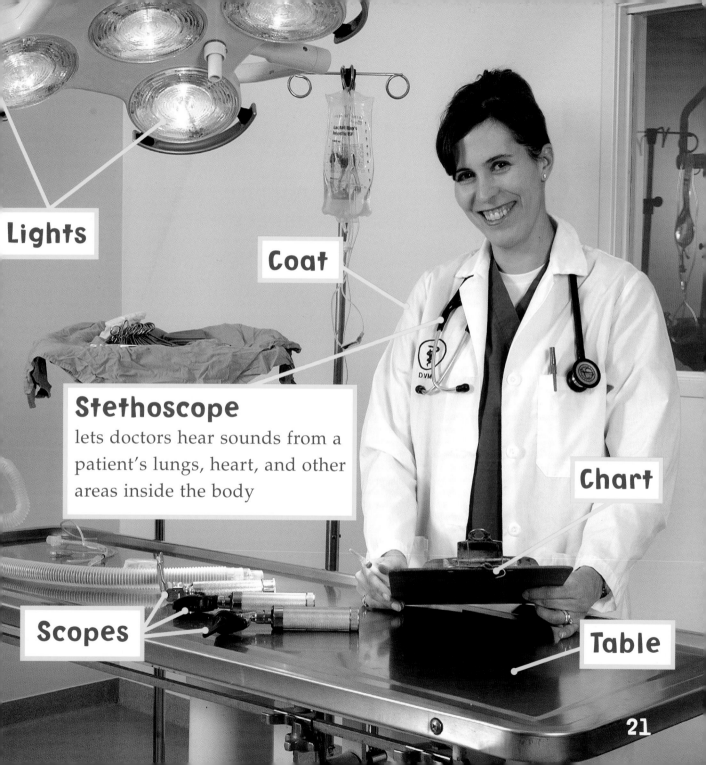

Lights

Coat

Stethoscope
lets doctors hear sounds from a patient's lungs, heart, and other areas inside the body

Chart

Scopes

Table

Glossary

appointment (uh-POINT-muhnt)—an agreement to meet at a certain time

clinic (KLIN-ik)—a building where medical care is given; veterinary clinics care for animals.

disease (duh-ZEEZ)—a sickness or illness

emergency (ee-MUR-juhn-see)—a sudden and dangerous situation

germs (JURMS)—small living things that cause diseases

operation (op-uh-RAY-shuhn)—medical treatment where the body is cut open

technician (tek-NISH-uhn)—someone who can work with lab equipment and tools

Read More

Englart, Mindi Rose. *A Veterinarian.* How Do I Become A. San Diego: Blackbirch Press, 2004.

Raatma, Lucia. *Veterinarians.* Community Workers. Minneapolis: Compass Point Books, 2003.

Riddle, John. *Veterinarian.* Careers with Character. Broomall, Penn.: Mason Crest Publishers, 2003.

Internet Sites

Do you want to find out more about veterinarians and pets? Let FactHound, our fact-finding hound dog, do the research for you!

Here's how:
1. Visit *http://www.facthound.com*
2. Type in the **Book ID** number: 0736822879
3. Click on **FETCH IT**.

FactHound will fetch Internet sites picked by our editors just for you!

Index